AF673302

SMART BRAIN RIGHT BRAIN

Let's Learn Coding

Om KIDZ
An imprint of Om Books International

First Published in 2021 by

Om KIDZ | Om Books International

Corporate & Editorial Office
A-12, Sector 64, Noida 201 301
Uttar Pradesh, India
Phone: +91 120 477 4100
Email: editorial@ombooks.com
Website: www.ombooksinternational.com

Sales Office
107, Ansari Road, Darya Ganj
New Delhi 110 002, India
Phone: +91 11 4000 9000
Email: sales@ombooks.com

Author: Shweta Sinha
Editor: Kirti Pathak
Art & Design: Anshuman Pandey, Gaurav Bhandari, Harish Arya

ISBN: 978-93-5276-839-4

Printed in India

10 9 8 7 6 5 4 3 2 1

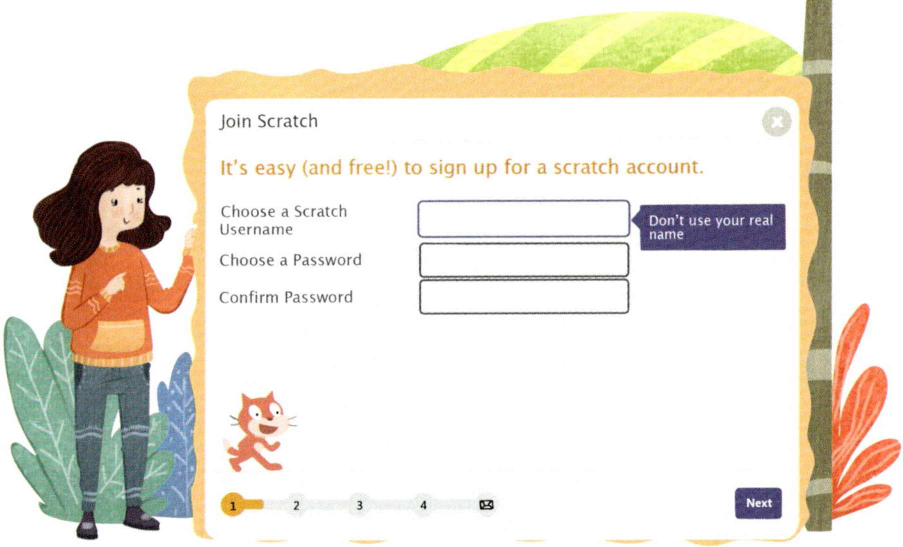

CONTENTS

1. What Is Coding?

Coding is another word for Computer Programming. A computer is just a box until you tell it what to do. Without your instructions, the computer will sit around doing nothing.

Description of Code

Code is simply a set of instructions that tells a computer to do something. What instructions would you give to a microwave so that it functions?

- If the door is open, turn off the microwave and switch on the lights.
- If the door is closed, switch off the interior lights.
- If a number button is pressed, add the number to 'time remaining to cook'.
- If the start button is pressed, turn on the microwave and rotate the turntable. Count down the 'time remaining to cook'.
- When 0:00 is the 'time remaining to cook', then turn off the microwave and sound an alarm.
- When the door is opened, turn off the microwave, turn off the alarm and reset.

POCKET FACT

Code also lets you play games, browse the web and share pictures with friends.

Computer Languages

Code allows you to speak with a computer in a language that both of you can understand. It is called a '**Programming Language**' or a '**Computer Language**'.

A code is written using specific rules; just like grammar. If you could write the instruction - 'If the door is open, turn off the microwave and switch on the lights' - in computer language, it would look something like this:

```
if (DoorIsOpen) {
microwave.off();
interiorLights.on();
}
else{
interiorLights.off();
}
```

DID YOU KNOW?

Lady Ada Lovelace wrote the world's first computer program.

How does Code work?

Computers work on electricity. They understand only the 'ON' and 'OFF' stages. 'ON' means there is a flow of current. 'OFF' means there is no flow of current. Computers are like a bunch of switches inside. The electronic components send signals by controlling the flow of the current.

'ON' signifies '1'.

'OFF' signifies '0'.

This is called the **binary code**. When we write a program, our words get converted into binary so the computer can understand them too.

POCKET FACT

We are surrounded by computer programs. Code controls every electronic device, including the calculator and the gaming console.

Binary Code

Every letter, number and symbol has an associated binary code. If the binary code for the letters B, A and N are:

Letter	B	A	N
Binary	01000010	01000001	01001110

Binary Digit

↓

1 10

Binary Number

Each individual '1' and '0' is called a binary digit.

How would you write 'BANANA' in binary?

Answer:

To a computer this sequence of 0's and 1's means 'BANANA'. Even 'banana' has a different sequence of numbers.

BANANA= 01000010 01000001 01001110 01000001 01001110 01000001

B A N A N A

The good news is that the computer languages we use to write code uses simple English words, not binary code.

I am a kid. What can I do with coding?

Coding is for anyone with a curious mind. Coding is not just for grownups and engineers. If you love to create new things, coding is for you. You can make your own website or create a new game. You can even make some music. Coding lets you build almost anything you can imagine on your computer.

DID YOU KNOW?

In the computer world "binary digit" is often shortened to the word "bit".

2. Let's Get Coding!

Let's create our very first computer program. Scratch is an easy-to-use tool to build your own stories, animations, games or artwork.

Setting up a Scratch account

Scratch can be used both online or offline. Using Scratch online needs an internet connection. Open the Scratch website by typing **https://scratch.mit.edu** on your web browser.

Click 'Join Scratch' to create an account. This opens up the sign-up wizard window:

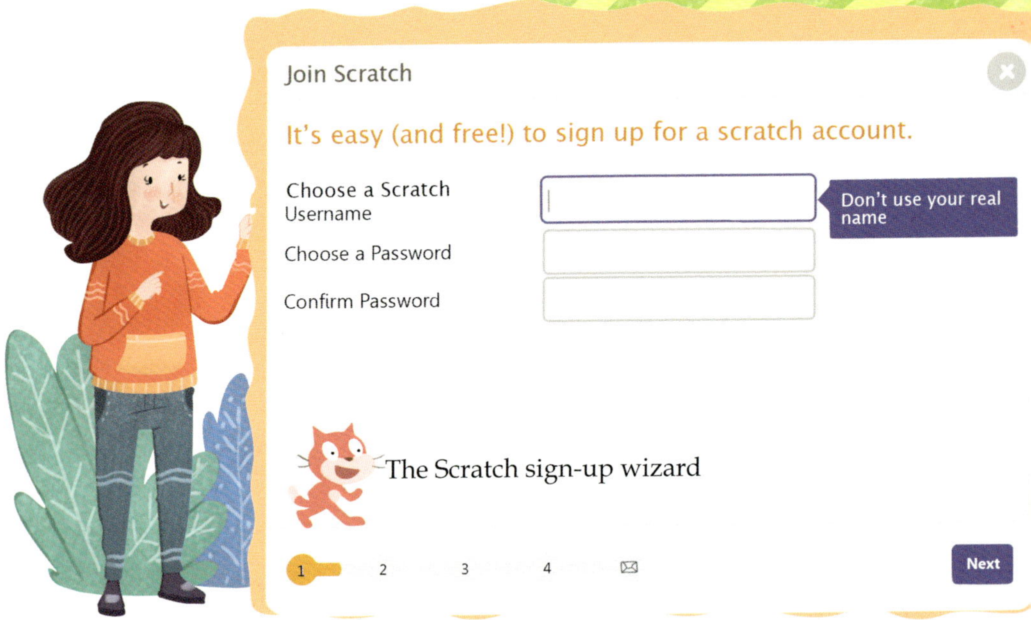

The Scratch sign-up wizard

Provide details asked for in the sign-up wizard. Don't use your real name as the user name. You will need to keep an email address handy. Ask a grown-up for help.

Scratch offline

You can also use Scratch in offline mode. Download the Scratch software by going to **https://scratch.mit.edu/download** on your web browser. Click on the Download button and then run the.exe file to install the Scratch software on your computer. Once installed, you do not need the internet to use the software.

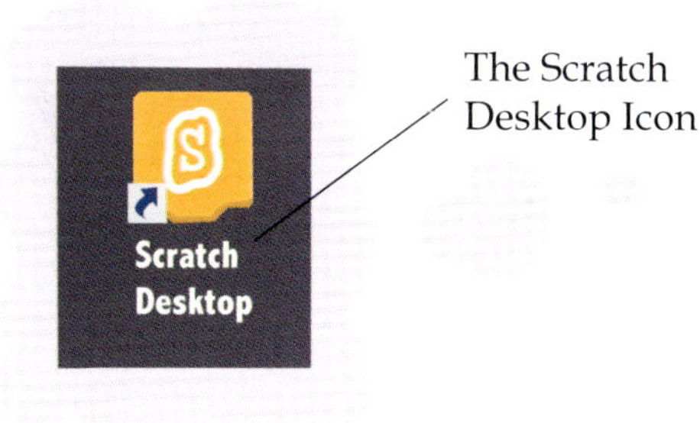

Online vs. Offline

While the Scratch website allows you to share your projects with other Scratch users, you cannot do so in the desktop version. In order to share your offline projects, login to the Scratch website and upload your projects into your account first.

POCKET FACT

Scratch is a free, visual programming tool. It is developed by the Lifelong Kindergarten Group at the MIT Media Lab.

The Scratch editor

Open the Scratch editor either by:

- Clicking on the 'Create' menu option on the Scratch website.
- Or double clicking the Scratch icon on your computer.

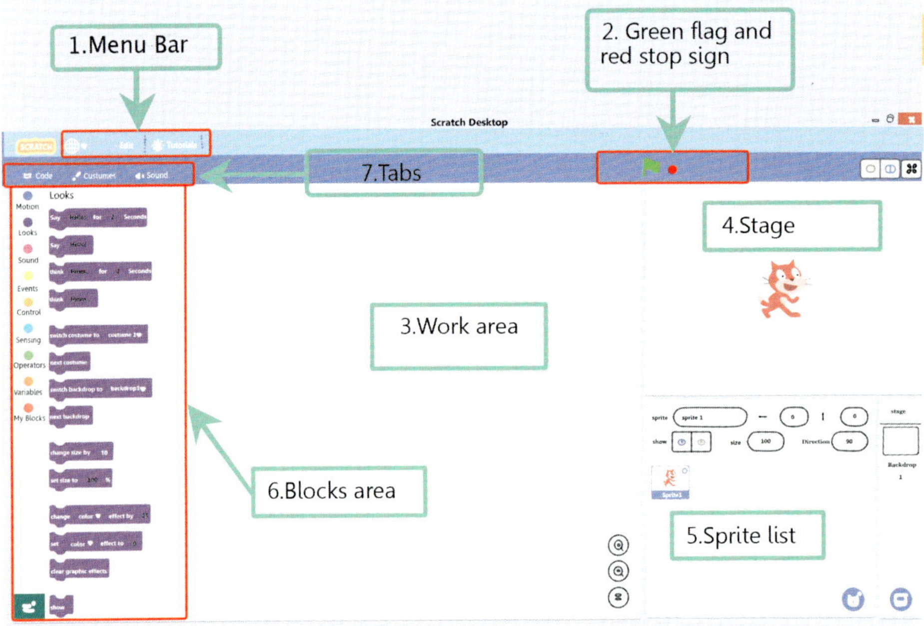

The Scratch Editor

Scratch uses code blocks that are puzzle-piece shapes used to perform an action. The work area is where you snap code blocks together to write computer programs called a script.

What You'll Learn:

- Using the Scratch editor.
- How to use Scratch to make a story.

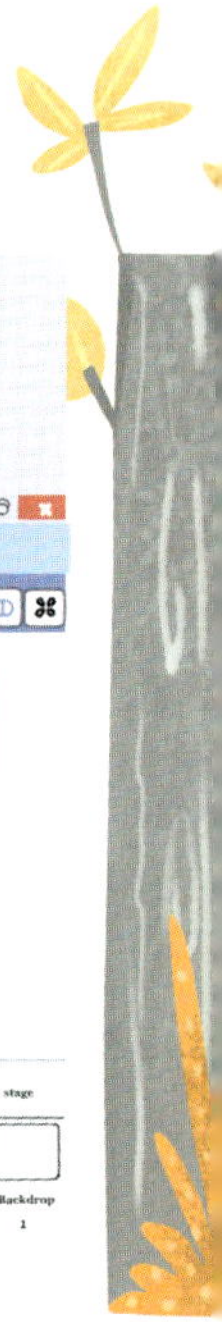

Code Blocks

Start coding by moving the coloured blocks around with your mouse. You can attach them vertically to each other to create code or scripts. The code blocks are organised by colour. There are code blocks for motion, looks, sound, events, etc.

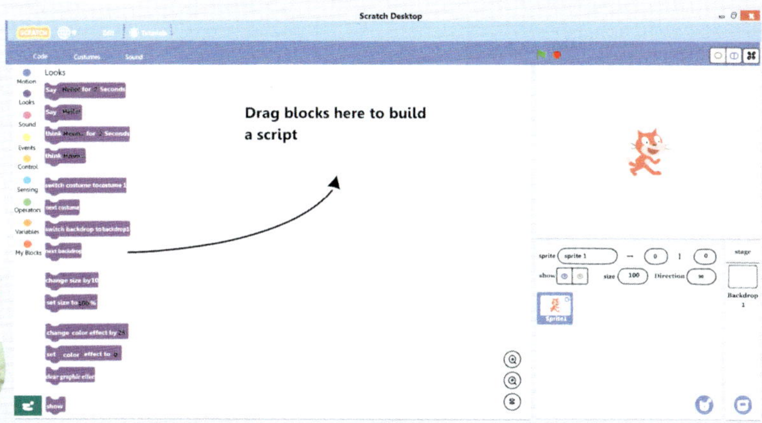

The friendly Scratch cat

You can see the cat sprite standing inside the 'stage' area. Are you ready to make the Scratch cat move and talk?

The Scratch cat sprite

POCKET FACT

Sprites are another name for the images you see on a Scratch editor screen. All Scratch programs have sprites and scripts that control them.

3. Your First Project

Step 1. Start a new script

We'll start by selecting an events block. Click on the yellow 'Events' label in the code block list.

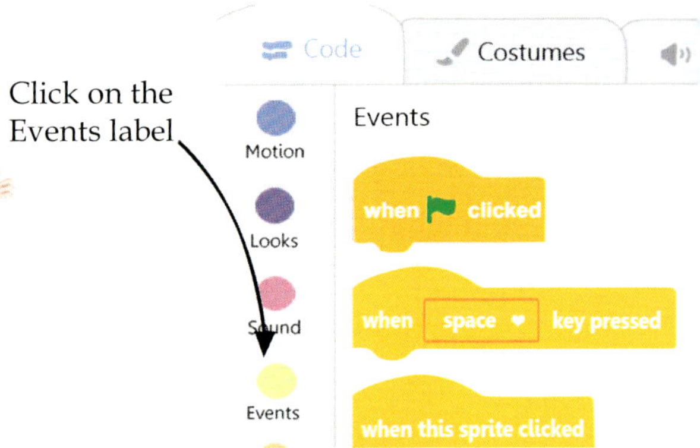

Step 2. Select an Events block

The list of blocks will scroll to show the events code blocks. Click the mouse on the topmost block and drag it to the work area.

Step 3. Select a Say block

Click on the purple 'Looks' label. Drag the topmost **Say Hello** block into the work area. Move it close to the events block so they snap together like a jigsaw puzzle.

Step 4. Make the cat move

Click on the blue 'Motion' label. Drag the topmost **move** block into the work area.

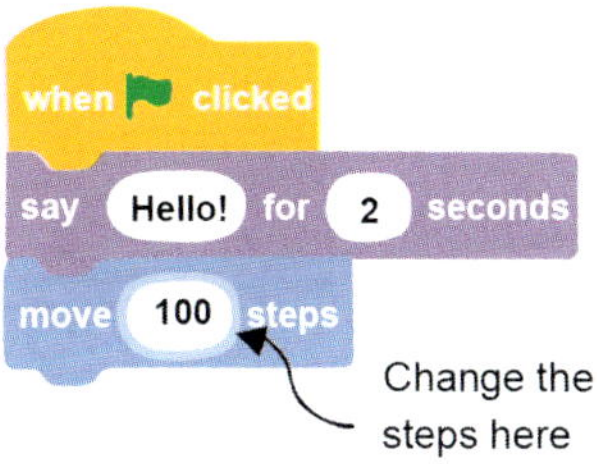

Step 5. Change the steps

Click on the move box and type '100' instead of '10'.

Step 6. Run the script

The script starts things off when we click the green flag. This is called 'running' the script.

Step 7. Your script in action

Click the green flag to see the cat say 'Hello' for 2 seconds, then move forward. The blocks work in the order you put them in.

Step 8. Save it

Good job creating your first computer program. Save your project by clicking on **File → Save to your computer**.

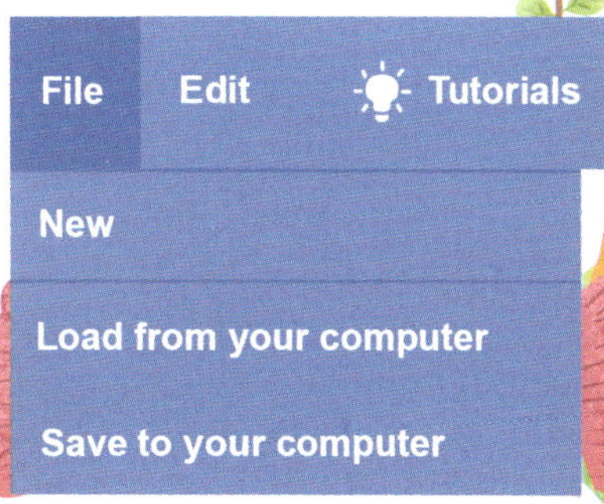

Coding Challenge:

Try adding other code blocks to your script and see how the Scratch cat behaves.

4. Again and Again

Sometimes we need to do an action again and again. Like when setting a table for four, you have to place a plate four times. Imagine telling someone to, "Set this plate, then set this plate, then set this plate, then set this plate." Wouldn't it be easier to just say "set these four plates"?

In the same way, we may need to repeat steps in our computer program. This is called a **loop**. Let's start a new project and try out **loops** with the Scratch cat.

Goal: Have the Scratch cat walk along a square shape.

Step 1. Select the actions to be repeated

- Drag the **move** block into the work area.
- Click the orange 'Control' label.
- Drag out the topmost **wait** block.
- Drag out the **turn** block.

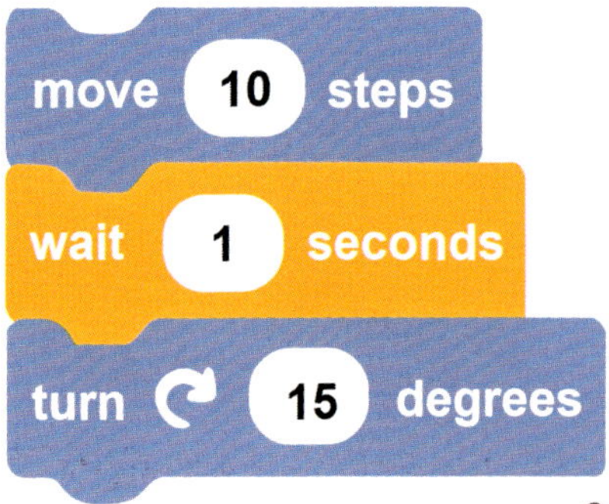

Step 2. Change the values

- Increase the number of steps to 100.
- Change the degree of turn to 90.

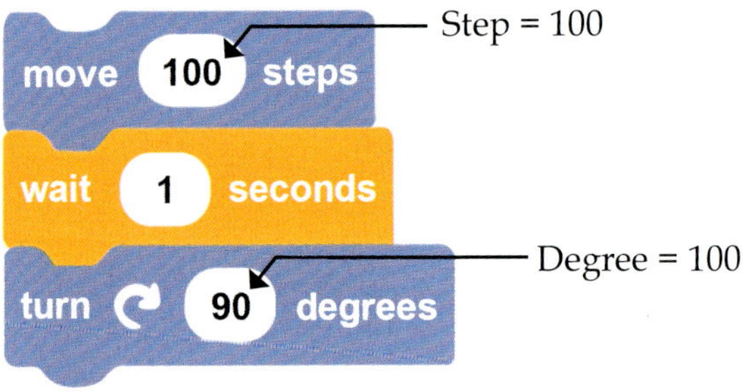

Step 3. Loop it

This code will make the cat walk 100 steps, take a 90 degree turn and stop. But we want it to repeat these steps 4 times to make a square. Drag out a **repeat** block from under 'Control'. Wrap the mouth of the **repeat** block around the other blocks. Change the **repeat** value to '4'.

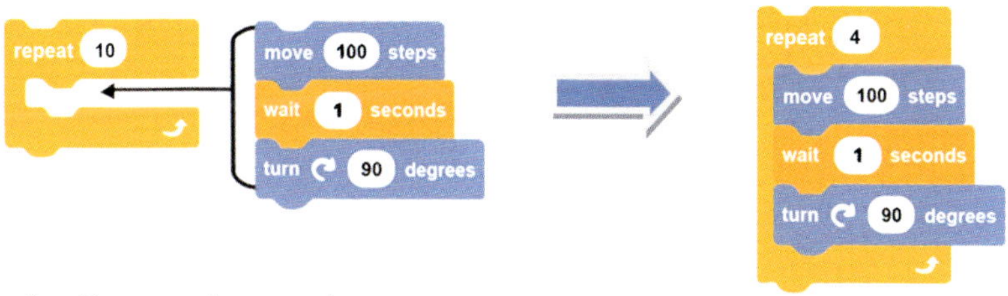

Step 4. Complete the script

Add the **green flag** event block on the top.

Step 5. Run the script

Click the green flag and watch the cat follow a square path.

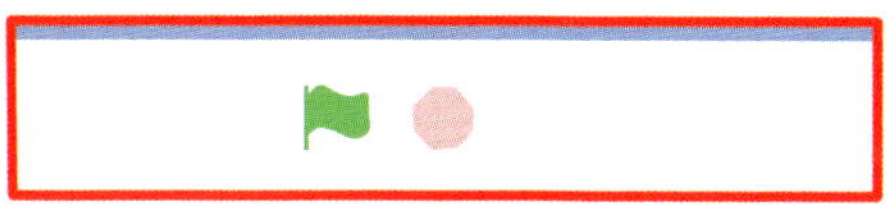

Coding Challenge:

Make the cat say 'Hello there!' for 2 seconds after every turn it takes.

Adding a backdrop

If the plain white stage behind the cat looks boring, you can change the backdrop.

- Click to select a new backdrop.

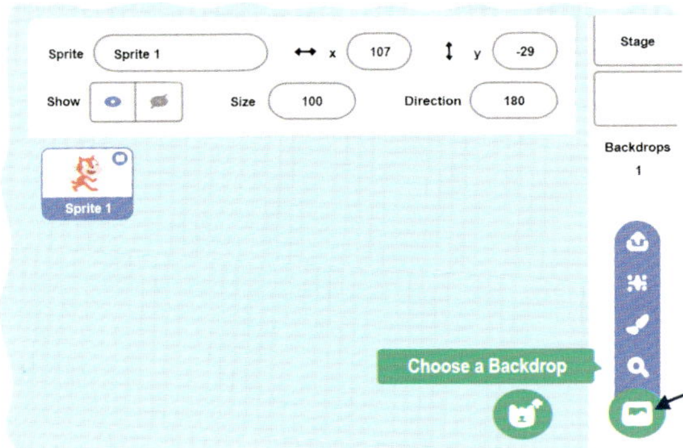

- This opens a library of backdrops to choose from. Click on any one of your choice.

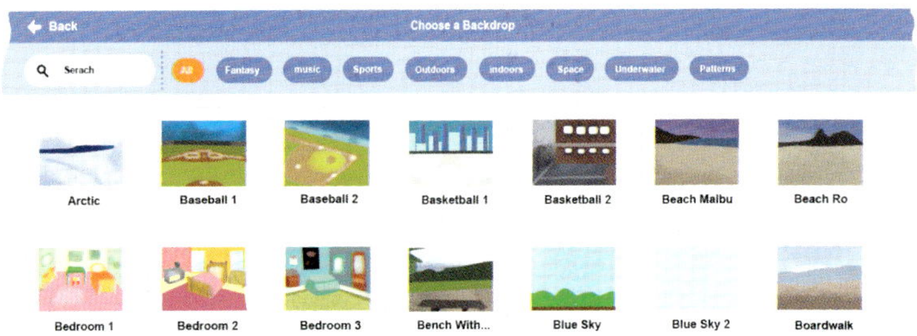

The Backdrop Library

- The selected backdrop now appears on the stage.

Coding Challenge:

Put the Scratch cat in a spotlight and make it meow there.
Hint: Use the backdrop search option to look for a spotlight.

Adding another Sprite

Every object in Scratch is a sprite. A sprite is another word for a graphic.

- Click to add a sprite to your program.

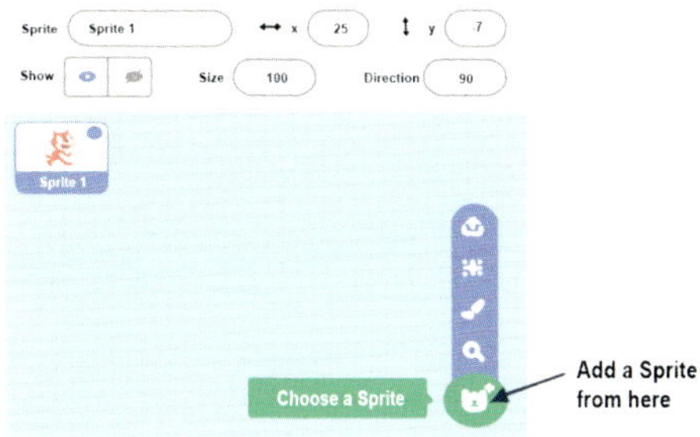

- This opens the sprite library to choose from. Click on any one of your choice.

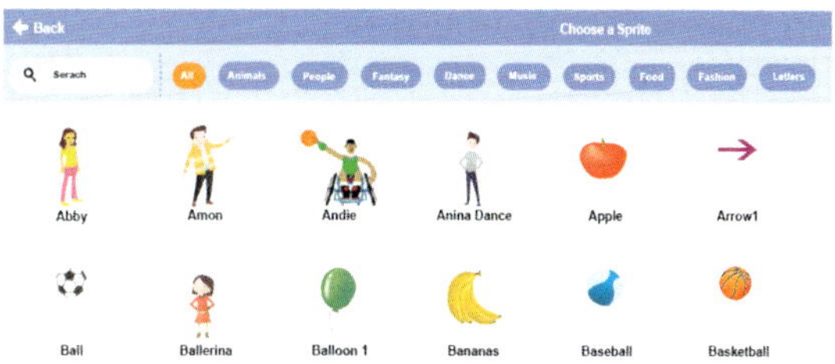

The Sprite Library

- The sprite appears in the stage area along with the cat.

- For each sprite, select it and write a separate set of code.
- To remove a sprite, right-click on its thumbnail, then click 'delete'.

POCKET FACT

You can paint , choose the surprise option or upload your images when adding backdrops or sprites.

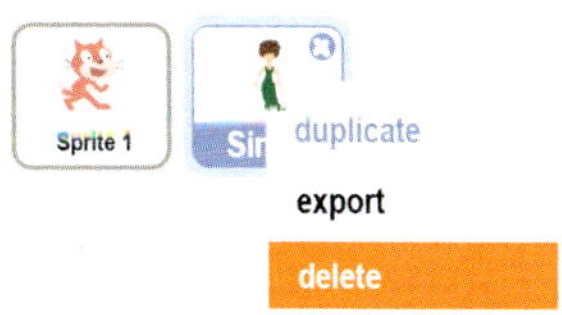

5. Animation

Cartoon characters in your favourite TV show are only a series of slightly different pictures. When you see the pictures in quick succession one after the other, it seems like a movement. This is called animation. You can animate sprites in the same way.

Costumes

Costumes are pictures of a sprite striking different poses. The Scratch cat has two different costumes to show. Start a new project and click the 'Costumes' tab to view them.

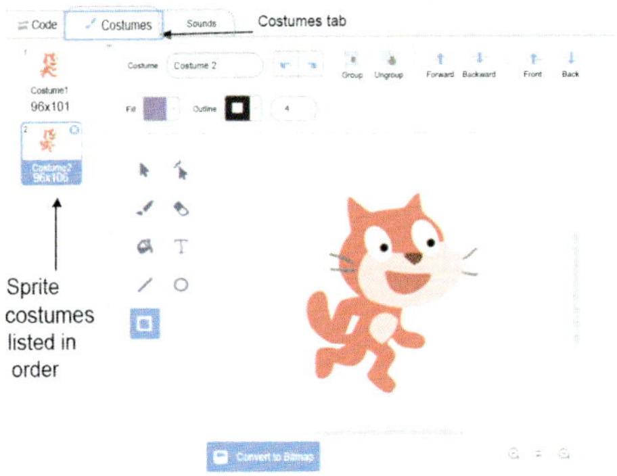

Walking the cat

1. Drag out the **forever** loop into the Work Area.

2. Inside the loop add:

- A **next costume** block from 'Looks' and
- A **wait .5 second** block from 'Control'.

3. Run the script. The picture of the cat changes every half second, making it appear as if it is walking.

Coding Challenge:

Add a **boardwalk** backdrop and make the cat walk forward on the boardwalk. Hint: You should add motion blocks to the script.

A flying bat

You can use the same code with other sprites too. Let us add the bat sprite to the project.

1. Open the Sprite Library.
2. Click on the **Animals** tab and select the **Bat** sprite.

The Sprite Library

3. Add the same costume changing script as before to the bat and watch it fly.

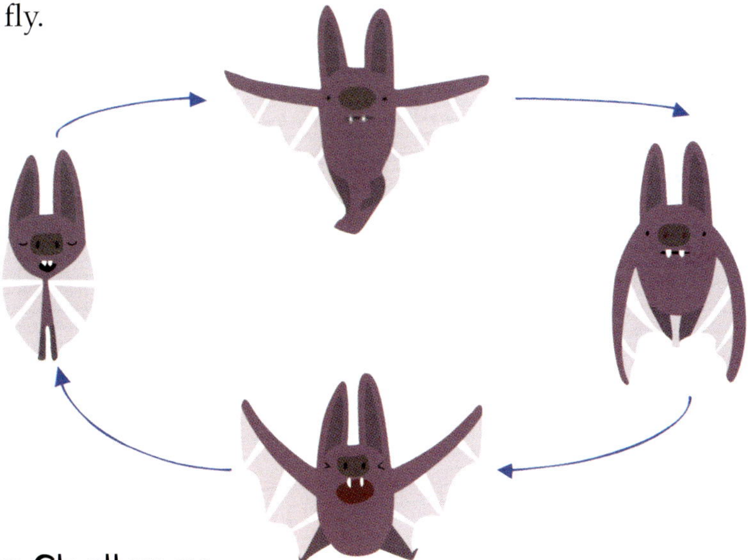

Coding Challenge:

Make the bat fly above the walking cat. Have a sprite party by adding other sprites in the same way. Add a cool backdrop for more fun.

A music and dance party

Music and friends are all you need for a dance party.

Let's gather friends

- Paint your own sprite - Draw a sprite to your liking. Give your sprite more costumes for more fun.

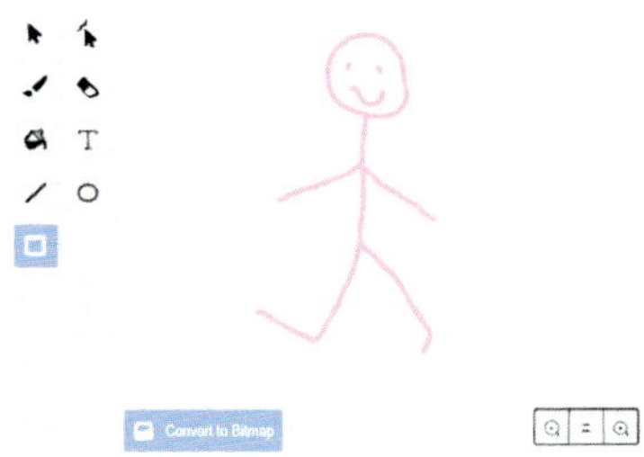

- Add a **Dance** sprite from the Sprite Library

Where's the music?

- Add a **Drum Kit** sprite and drag out Sound blocks for the Drums.

The Stage

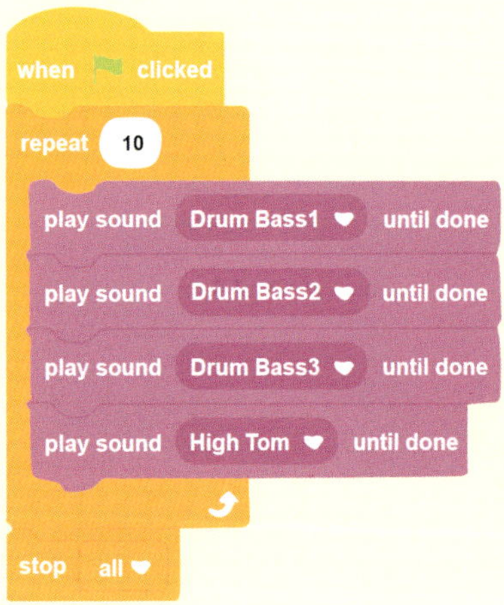

Let's party!

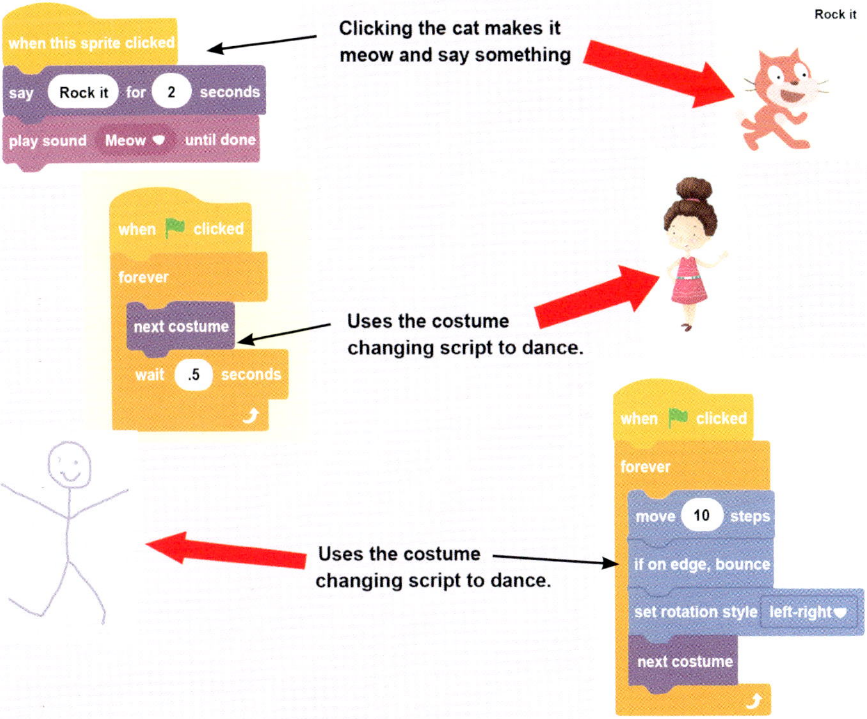

Tip: Stop the animation by clicking the red Stop Button anytime.

6. Math with Scratch

The Scratch cat can solve math problems too. Some math symbols may appear different from the ones you use, but that is only to fit them with the symbols on a computer keyboard.

Math Tools

Everything to do with math is under the green 'Operators' label. These four blocks look familiar, don't they?

• **Add (+)**	• **Subtract (-)**
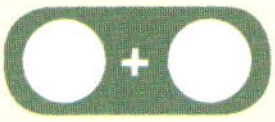 This block adds the numbers in the two windows.	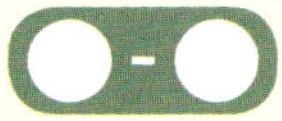 This block finds the difference between the numbers in the two windows.
• Multiply (*)	• **Divide (/)**
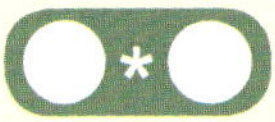 Multiplies the two numbers. Since 'x' resembles the letter, '*' is used as the multiplication symbol.	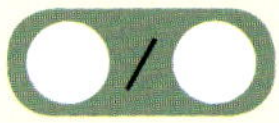 Divides the first number by the second. Since the keyboard does not have the division symbol, '/' is used instead.

Using the operators

To use the math blocks, place them inside a **say** block.

Solving Problems

If Peter has to divide 45 candy bars amongst his 9 friends, he can use the following code to calculate the answer.

He can also solve this problem using variables:

Step 1: Create variables to work with

Click the dark orange 'Variables' label. Click on **Make a Variable** and create a variable 'candy bars'. Repeat for a second variable, 'friends'.

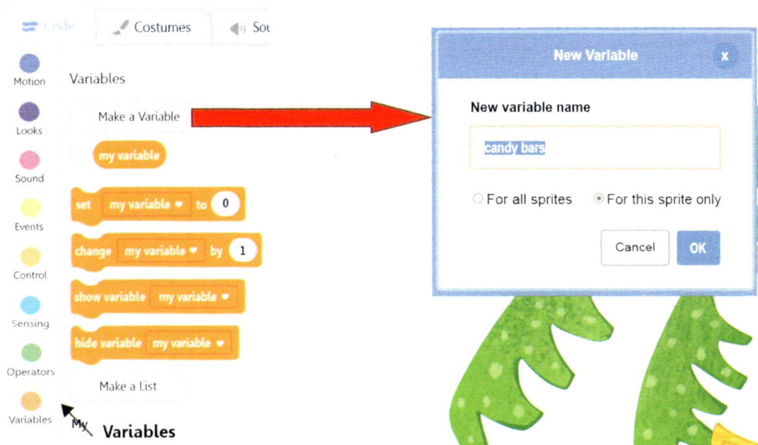

Step 2. Code using the variables

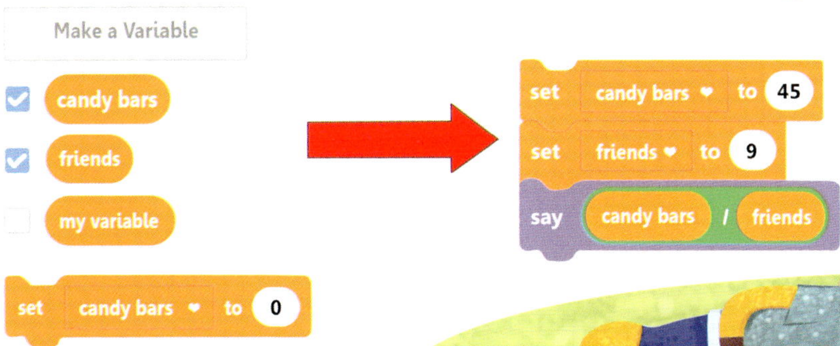

Coding Challenge:

Use variables to add two numbers, find their difference, multiply them and divide them.

7. Game: Dodge the Ball

Balls are falling from the sky. Help Giga escape the falling balls.

The Setup

• Sprites- Remove the cat and add **Giga Walking** and the **Ball**.

• Backdrop- Choose **Blue Sky**.

• Select Giga in the sprites list and change its size to '60'. Resize the Ball to '80' in the same way.

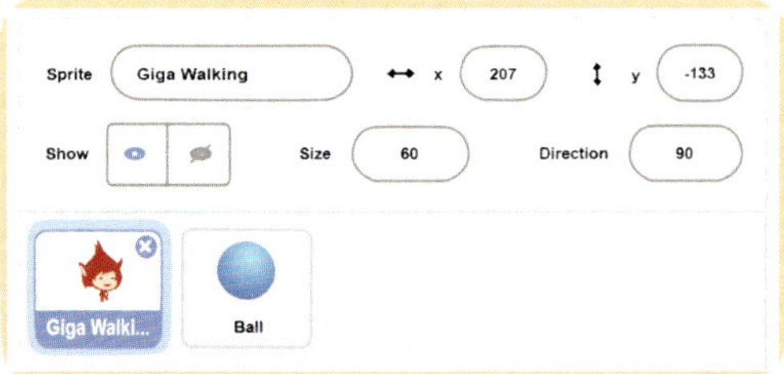

Set the ball rolling down

This sequence of code starts with the ball on the top and makes it fall down gradually. It repeats again and again until the game ends.

• Fix an initial position of the ball in the sky.

• Start a forever loop.

• Keep changing the y-value to make the ball fall down.

• If the ball touches the ground, put it back on the top by changing the x and y values and restart.

• Also change the costume to have some fun with coloured balls.

Get Giga walking

The arrow keys control Giga. She moves left and right to avoid the ball.

- Set the initial position of Giga on the ground.
- Start a forever loop.
- If the right arrow key is pressed then move Giga forward.
- If the left arrow key is pressed, move Giga backwards.
- The **next costume** block animates Giga.
- Game ends (**stop all**) if Giga touches the ball.

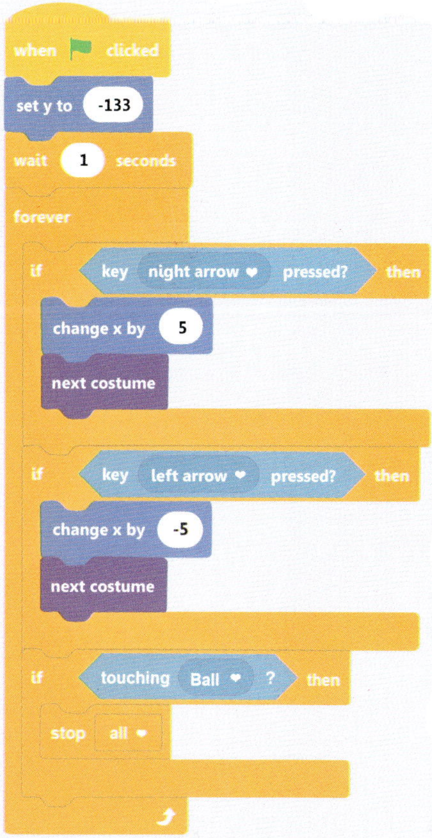

Enjoy the game

Coding Challenge: " Explore the Tutorials section on Scratch or go to https://scratch.mit.edu/explore/projects/all for more programming ideas.

8. Python

Now that you've enjoyed programming with Scratch, you are ready for bigger challenges. Python is a popular Programming Language that is simple and easy-to-use. With Python you can do everything you did in Scratch and more. You can build desktop software, web applications, mobile apps and even do complex scientific computing.

Can you guess which of these below have been developed using Python?

YouTube Google Dropbox Instagram

Answer: All of them!

Installing Python

Visit www.python.org/download to download and install Python on your computer. After installing, look for the Python IDLE in your application list and open it. It opens a window like this:

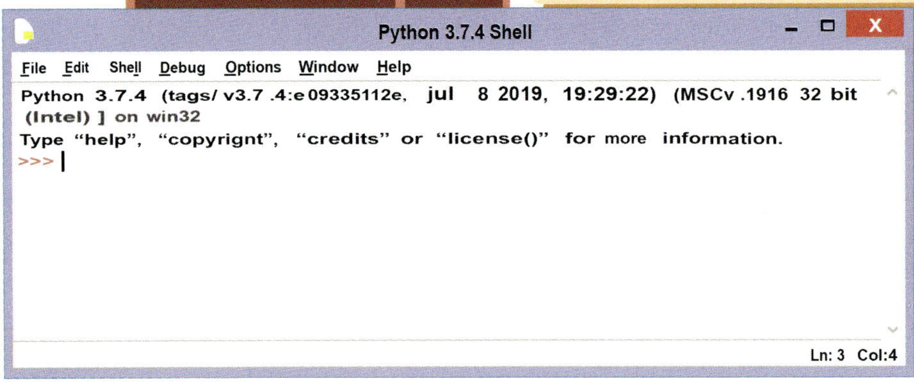

This is the Python Shell. The sign '>>>' is called the prompt. Type the following command at the prompt:

```
>>> print("Hello World")
```

Press enter to see this output:

```
>>> print ("Hello world")
Hello World
>>> |
```

Congratulations! You just typed in your first Python code. Notice that the prompt reappears after the output, waiting for your next command.

Save it

Click on **File→New File** from the top menu. This opens an empty window with 'untitled' on the top bar. Type your Python command here:

```
print("Hello") |
```

Use **File → Save** to save your file. Give a filename when prompted to. Now choose **Run→ Run Module**. You should see this:

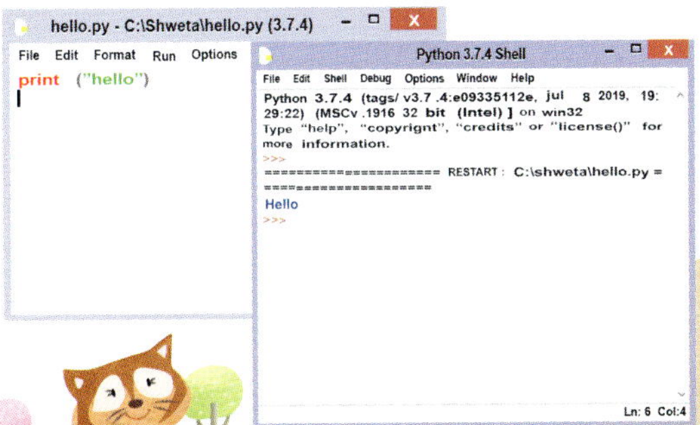

What you learnt

You learnt to start off with a simple Python program. You can learn more Python commands and build bigger programs.

Let's Get Active

Match the Scratch

Match the code block to the correct Scratch behaviour.

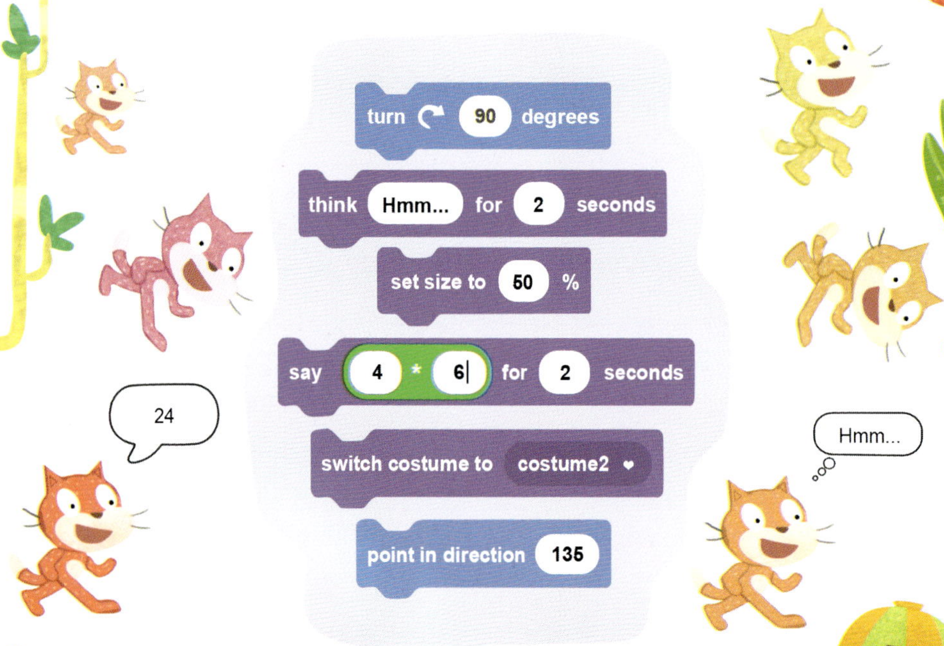

Hint: Try these code blocks in your Scratch Editor.

What do you know?

1. A ____________ is a different picture a sprite can show on the stage.
   (a) Selfie (b) Costume
   (c) Photo (d) Cartoon

2. ______________ is showing slightly different pictures to make a sprite appear to move.
   (a) Movie (b) Video
   (c) Animation (d) Dance

3. Python is a ______________ .
   (a) Snake (b) Computer Language
   (c) Script (d) Shell

4. Which Block would you put inside the cat's **forever** loop to make it look like it is walking?
   (a) Next Costume (b) Say Hello!
   (c) Next Backdrop (d) Hide

5. What Python command will you use to display "Hello there!" on the screen?
   (a) display ("Hello there!")
   (b) show ("Hello there!")
   (c) print ("Hello there!")

6. What window does the Python IDLE open?
   (a) Screen (b) Sheet
   (c) Shell (d) Editor

Math Time

1. What answers will the computer give for these math blocks?

45 + 67	67 - 49	13 * 10	75 / 5

2. Using these variables, find out the values of the blocks:

```
set a to 10
set b to 4
```

3 * b	a / 5	b + 7	a - b

3. What will the cat say?

say letter 1 of apple	
say length of apple	
say 1 > 50	
say join apple banana	